# THIS COLORING BOOK

*BELONGS TO*

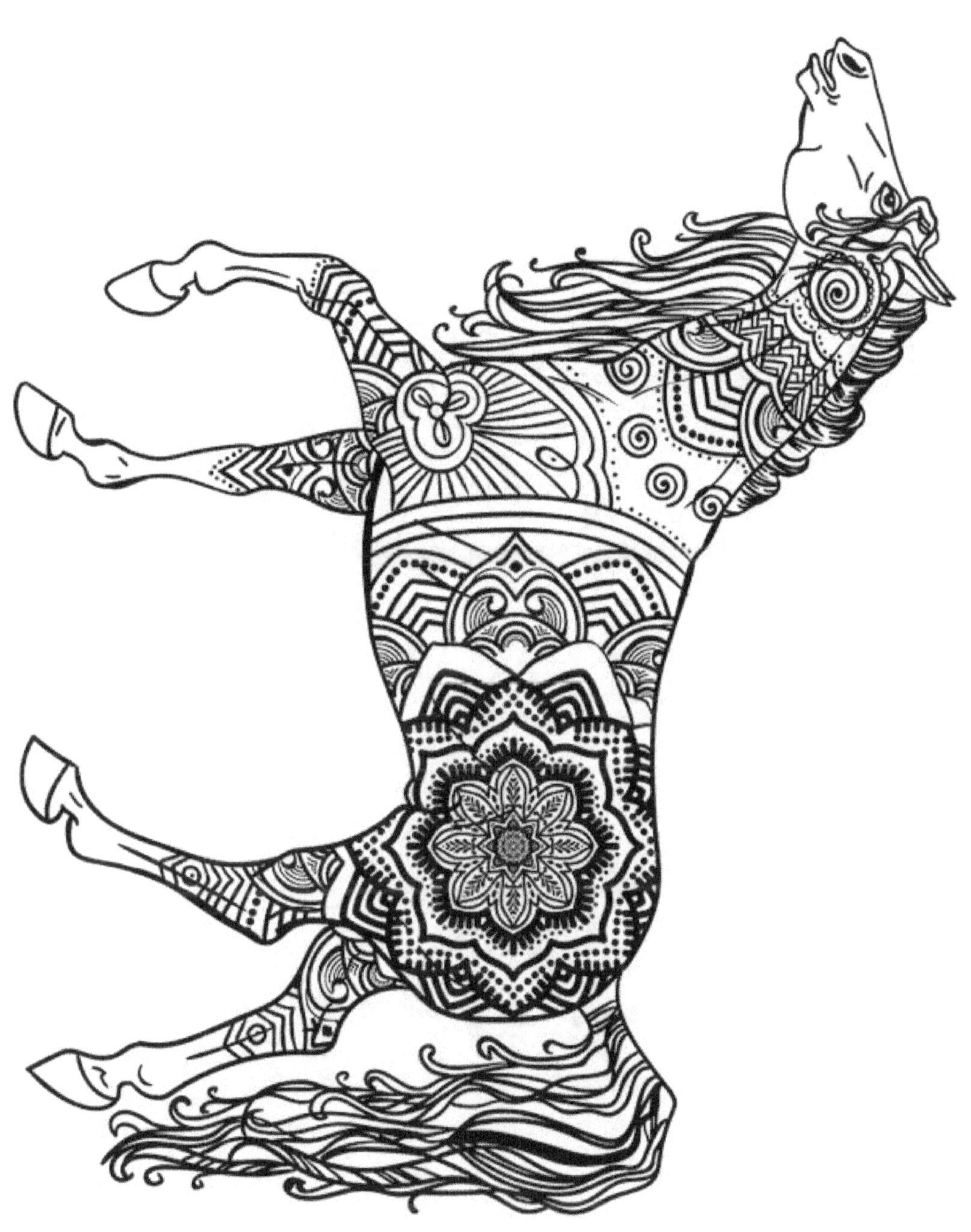

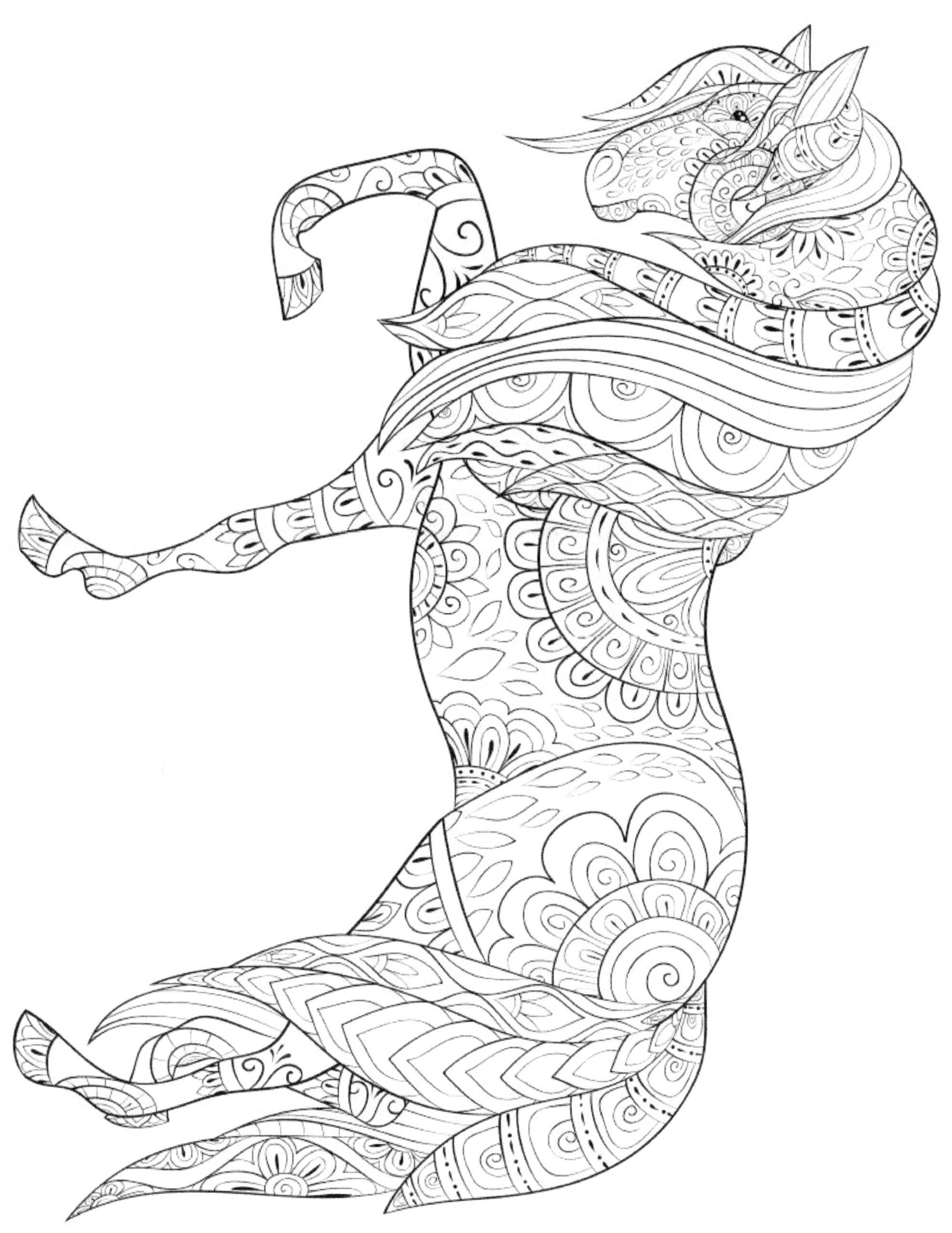

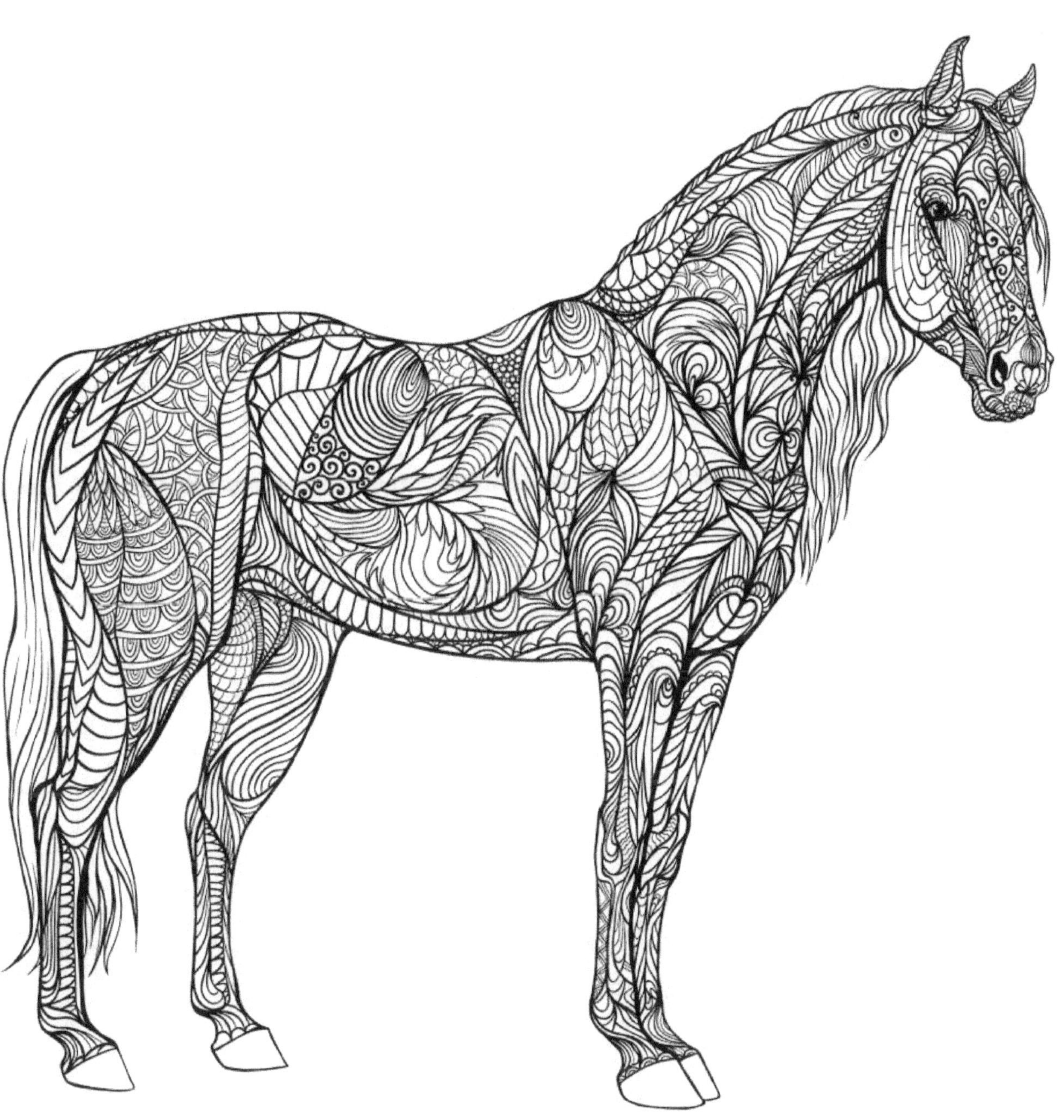

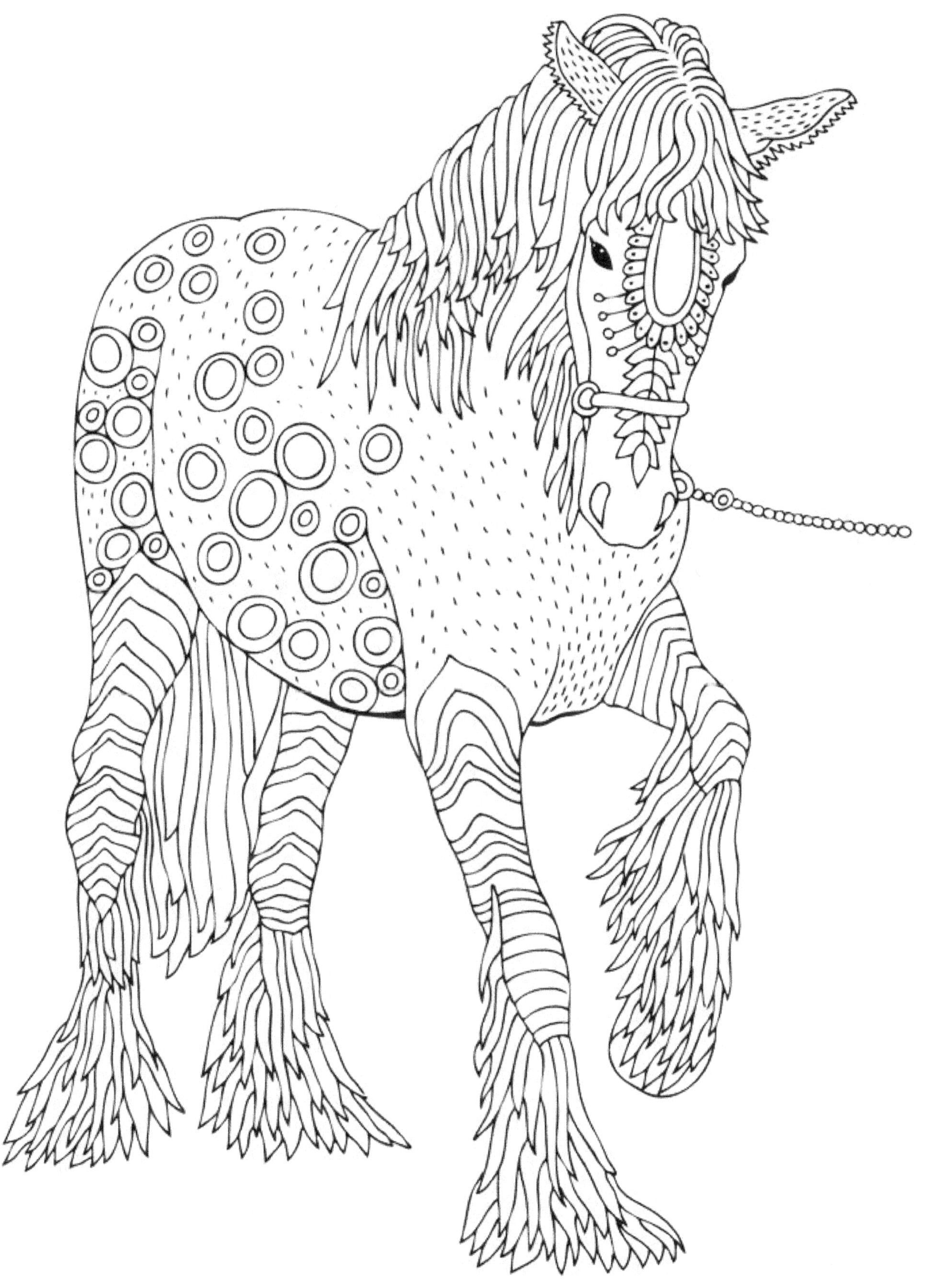

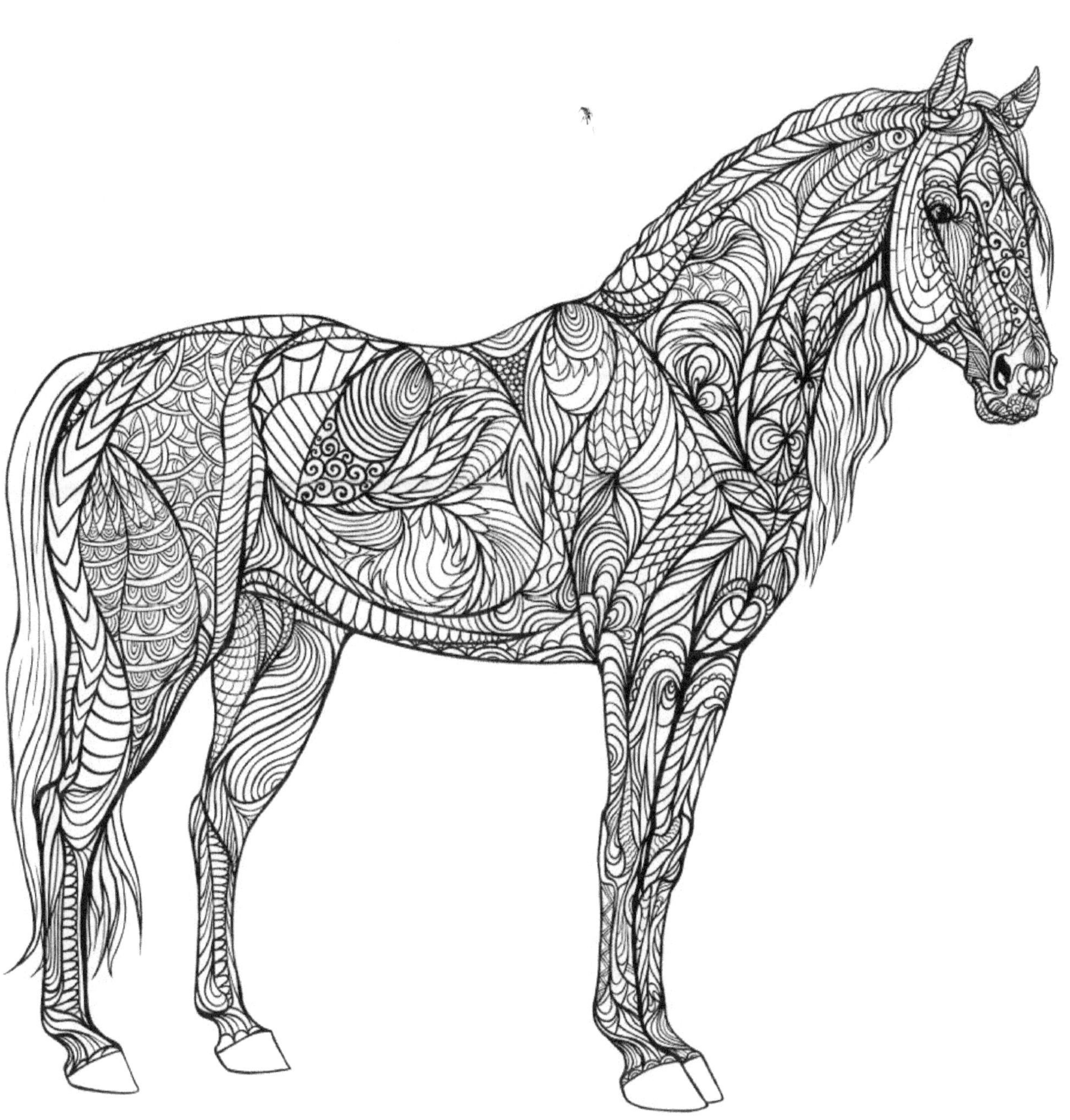

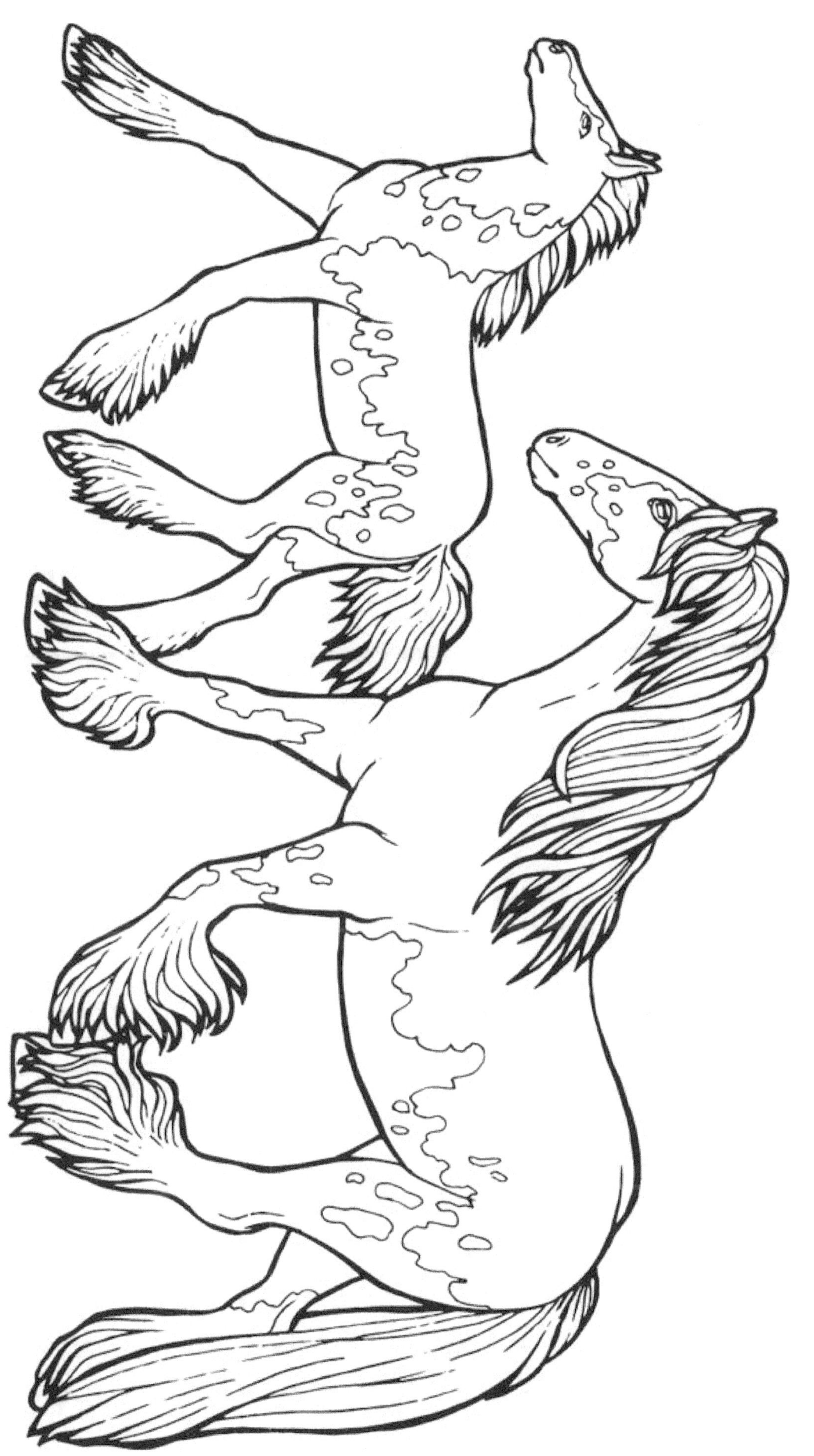

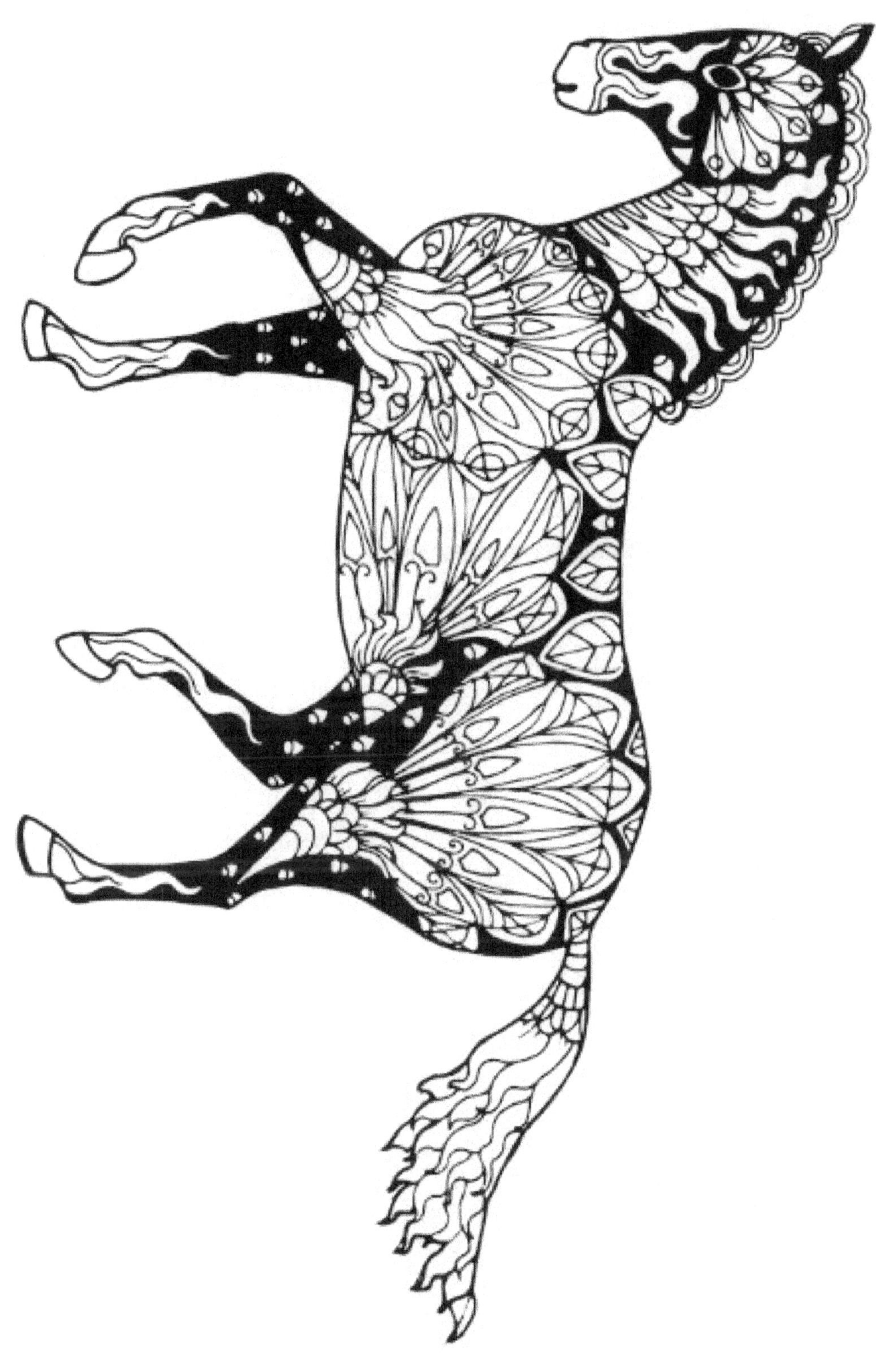

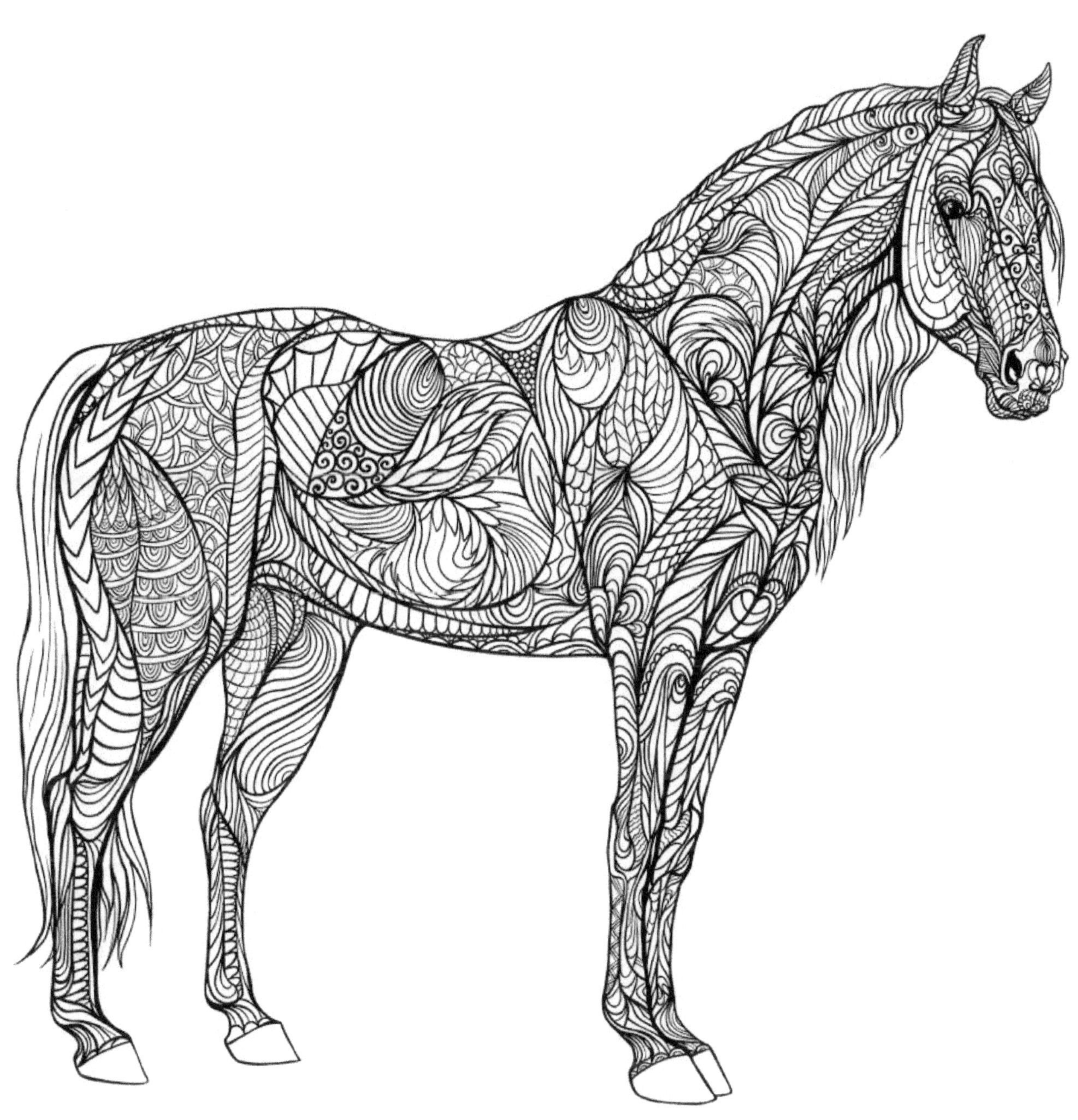

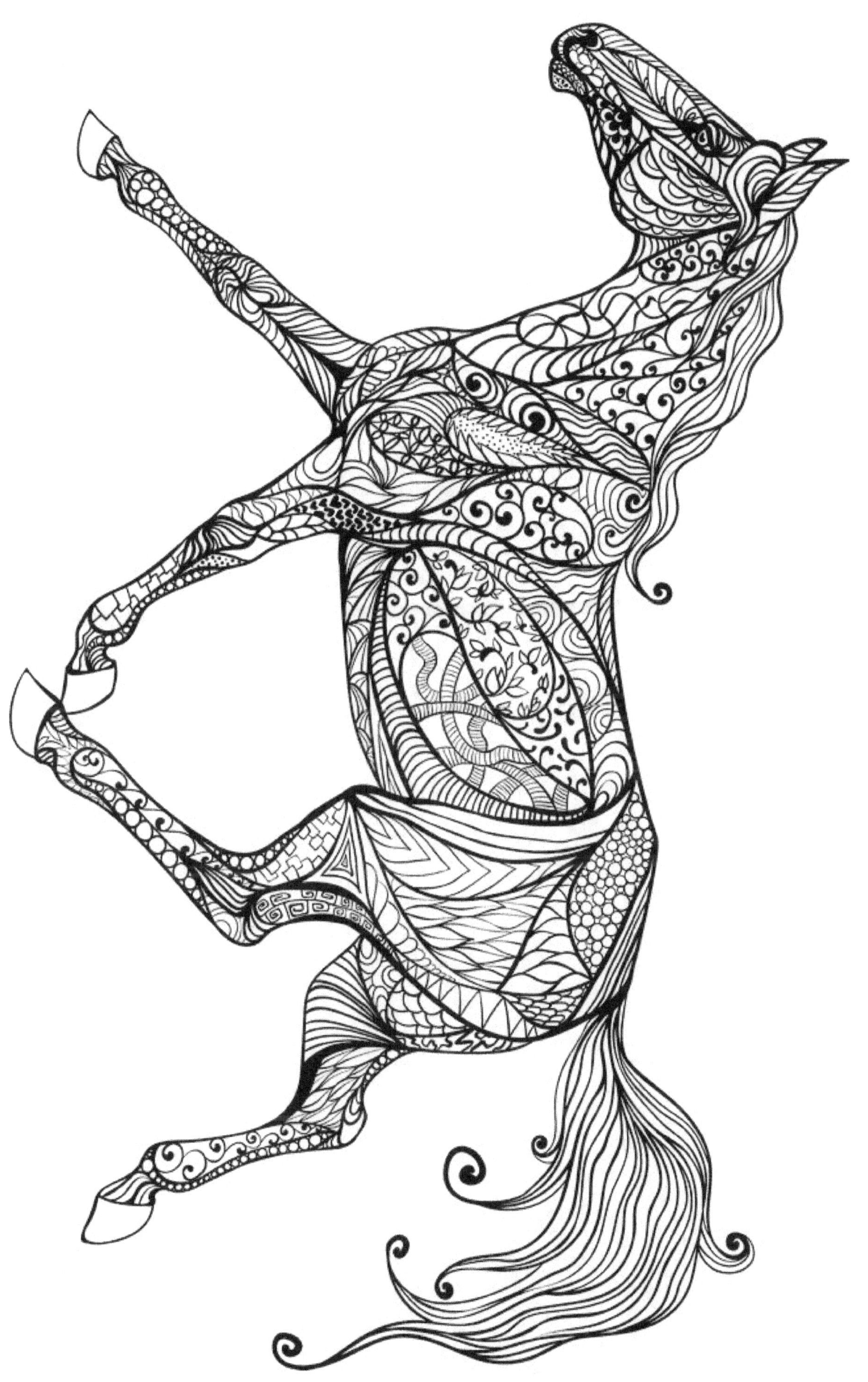

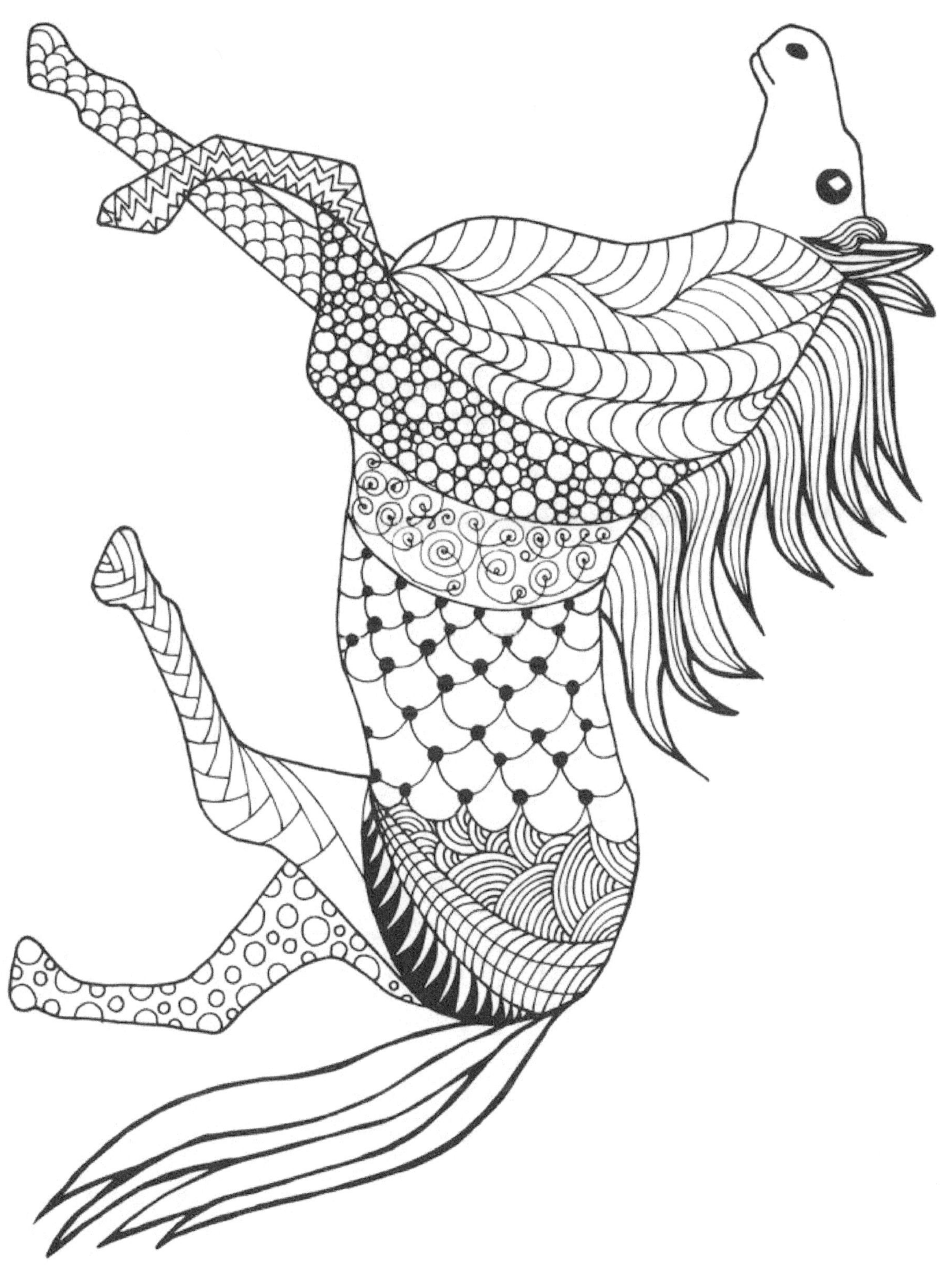

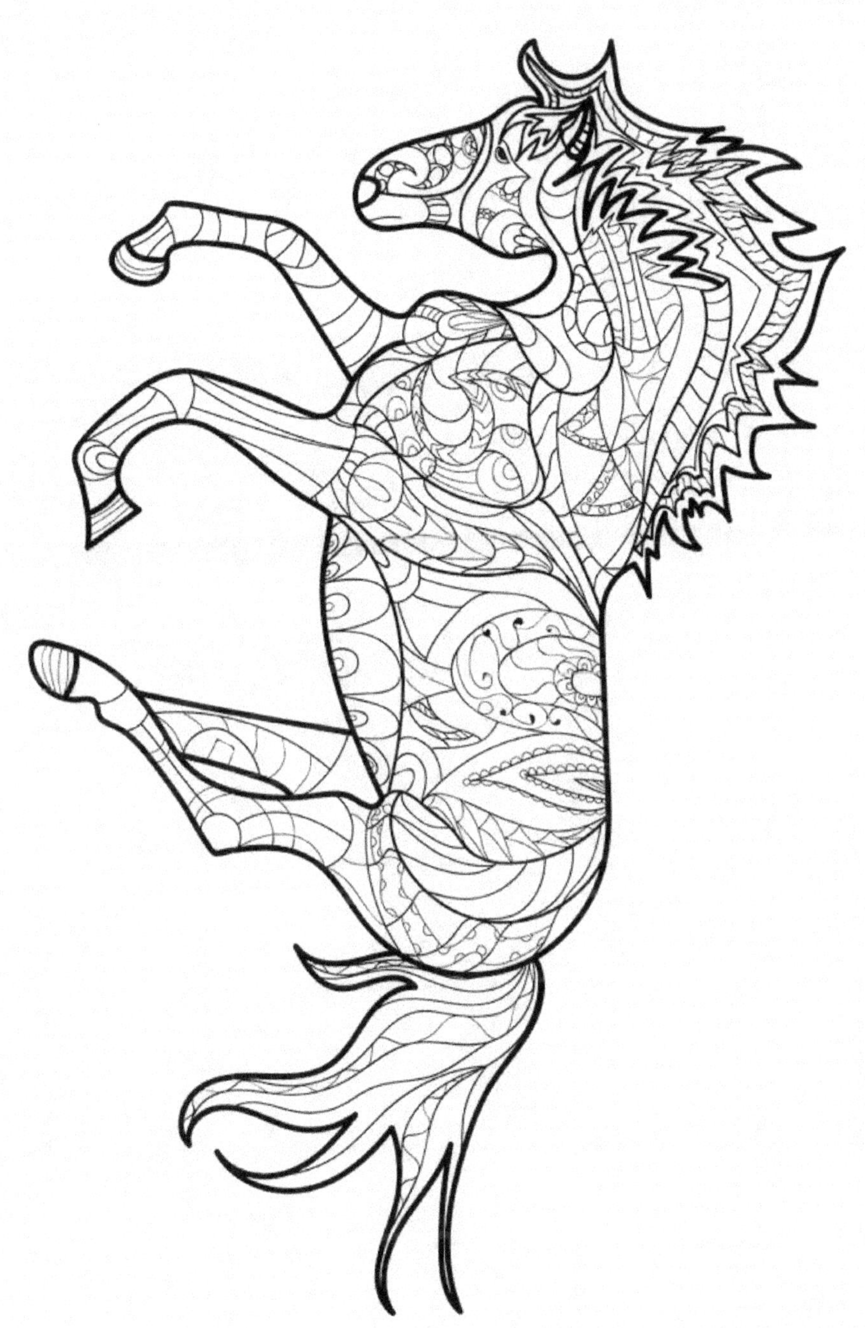